GOLFER'S COMPANION

GOLFER'S COMPANION

MICHAEL HOBBS

Sebastian Kelly

This edition first published in 1997 by Sebastian Kelly
2 Rectory Road
Oxford OX4 1BW

© Anness Publishing Limited 1997

Produced by Anness Publishing Limited

ISBN 1 901688 30 5

A CIP catalogue record for this book is available from the British Library

The majority of pictures in this book were kindly supplied by
Michael Hobbs Golf Collection

Publisher: Joanna Lorenz
Project Editor: Fiona Eaton
Editor: Marion Paull
Additional Text: Steve Newell and Paul Foston
Techniques Photographer: David Cannon
Designer: Bet Ayer
Jacket Designer: Andrew Heath

Printed in Singapore

3 5 7 9 10 8 6 4 2

CONTENTS

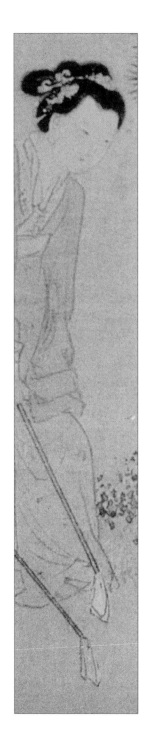

A BRIEF HISTORY OF GOLF

The origins of golf will certainly never be known. Many variations of stick-and-ball games were probably developing all over the world at different times and independently of each other, depending on climate and terrain.

A golf-like game called "colf" was played in the Netherlands from the thirteenth century until the early eighteenth when it was superseded by a more contained version. In colf there was no defined course. The game was played across country, aiming at prearranged targets such as church doors or trees. In winter it was played on frozen lakes, aiming at a peg.

At this time, the Netherlands was a great maritime and trading nation, her ships sailing the world, and the game travelled along with the goods across international boundaries. It is known that colf was played in Italy, Germany and probably the Dutch East Indies. There is also evidence of a form of it being played in Albany, New York, in 1659. The Netherlands had strong links with Scotland and it is quite likely that similar games evolved separately in the two countries and influenced each other.

In Scotland, the popularity of the game of "gowf" or "goff" is first evidenced by a royal decree of 1457 by which James II banned both "fute-ball" and golf because they were distracting his archers from practice – he

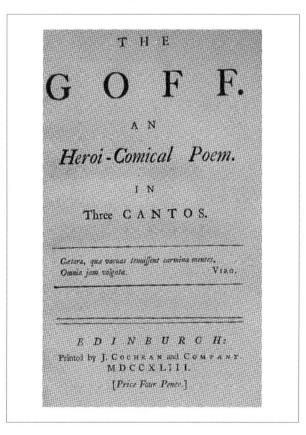

LEFT: The first written reference to golf came in 1457 when James II banned the game because he wanted his Scottish archers to practise "schuting" to use against the English, who had been successful in the battles of Crécy and Agincourt as a result of their skill with the longbow. The section illustrated here is from the first printed reference to golf in the Black Acts of 1566, so-called because of the heavy black type in which they were printed.

LEFT: This four-penny publication was the first to be entirely devoted to golf.

RIGHT: In the Netherlands, colf was also a winter game played on ice. This scene formed the decoration on an old Dutch tile.

BELOW: The "Gloucester colfer" is a detail from the great east window of Gloucester cathedral. The window, made to commemorate the battle of Crécy, dates from about 1350 and shows that a form of golf was being played in England even then.

wanted them to hone their skills to use against the hated English. It seems that the edict was not effective because in the same century two further bans were issued, the last in 1491. Alas

for archery, these efforts were abandoned when, after the Treaty of Glasgow brought peace between England and Scotland in 1501, James IV of Scotland took up the game himself. When James VI of Scotland also became King of England in 1603, he took the Scottish version of the game to London.

There is not much evidence of how the game developed during the seventeenth century. The precise rules of the game the Scots played then are not known, although in 1687 Thomas Kincaid, an Edinburgh man, recorded his thoughts on playing the game in a poem that amounted to the first written instructions. What is clear is that the game was not for the ordinary citizen because it was

A Poem by Thomas Kincaid, 1687

Gripe fast, stand with your left leg first not farr;
Incline your back and shoulders, but beware
You raise them not when back the club you bring:
Make all the motion with your bodie's swinge
And shoulders, holding still the muscles bent;
Play slowly at first till you the way have learnt
At such lenth hold the club as fitts your strenth,
The lighter head requires the longer lenth.
That circle wherein moves your club and hands
At forty-five degrees from the horizon stands
What at on stroak to effectuat you dispaire
Seek only 'gainst the nixt it to prepare.

expensive. The balls in use at the time each cost three times as much as a club and several were needed per game.

The golf club of the Company of Gentlemen Golfers – later called the Honourable Company of Edinburgh Golfers – was founded at Leith in 1744 with a clubhouse and the first known written rules of play. From the mid-eighteenth century to the later years of the nineteenth, however, the game declined. It was no longer encouraged at Court, George III, William IV and the young Queen Victoria having no particular interest in it, though William presented a medal to the Golf Club of St Andrews and conferred its title "Royal and Ancient" in 1834. However, a hard core of enthusiasts brought their organizational skills to bear and for the first time clubs were formed with their own premises. Rules were formulated, notably by the golf club of St

LEFT: Jeu de mail, a golf-like game, involved hitting the ball through a hoop. It was also called pele mele and the biggest court in Europe, 1000 yards long, was in London on the site of the street now called Pall Mall. This illustration is from a 1717 French book of rules of the game.

BOTTOM LEFT: References to the efforts made to stop the Scots playing golf on Sundays may be found in parish records. The game was banned on that day, and those playing golf instead of going to church were fined. The Old Course at St Andrews is still closed on Sundays, but these days it is to benefit the course rather than the players' souls.

BOTTOM RIGHT: Alexander McKellar, nicknamed "Cock o' the Green", was renowned for his passion for golf. This eighteenth-century Edinburgh innkeeper became so obsessed with the game that he played after dark by the light of a lantern and his wife even brought his meals to the course.

Andrews in Scotland. The Scottish and English representatives of large commercial companies and those in the employ of the colonial service took the game abroad with them, to India, Australia, Canada and, of course, America. David Deas of Charleston, South Carolina, was originally from Leith in Scotland. In 1743 he ordered 96 golf clubs and 432 balls. The bill of lading for this shipment still exists. In 1750 and 1751, 72 clubs and 576 balls were sent from Glasgow to Virginia and in 1765, 18 clubs and 144 balls from Glasgow to Maryland. Other contemporary records show that golf was being played in 1779 in New York, 1786 in South Carolina and 1795 in Georgia.

LEFT: "William Inglis on Leith Links" (detail) by David Allan (c.1787). William Inglis was captain of the Honourable Company of Edinburgh Golfers from 1782–84. The procession headed by the silver club can be seen in the background.

FAR LEFT: When the Gentlemen Golfers were founded in 1744, the city of Edinburgh donated a silver club to be competed for each year. The winner became the "Captain of the Golf" and was obliged to attach a silver ball to the club. The competition was announced each year by parading the club with its growing number of silver balls attached through the city. The tradition has continued and now the Edinburgh Golfers have four silver clubs adorned with a multitude of silver balls kept at their club-house at Muirfield.

THE ROYAL AND ANCIENT GOLF CLUB OF ST ANDREWS

The members of the Company of Gentlemen Golfers often played at Musselburgh a few miles away, which had a links course, or made the longer trip to St Andrews, which had a better one. When the St Andrews club was formed in 1754 it was supported by the Gentlemen Golfers. Its thirteen rules of play were virtually identical. These rules were adopted by most other clubs throughout the country, including Blackheath.

RIGHT: Caddies have probably been around since the game began. Until 1880 they had to carry all the clubs and other equipment loose, as golf bags were not invented until then. This is one of the more eccentric characters to fill the role, William Gunn, known as "Caddy Willie", painted by C.H. Robertson in 1839. He liked to wear lots of jackets and it's said that he also wore at least three pairs of trousers at a time.

LEFT: The 4th at St Andrews about 1890. There was traditionally a stop here for ginger beer and so it became known as the Ginger Beer hole.

BELOW: Royal Blackheath, formed in 1766, was the first golf club in England, though golf had been played on the Heath since James VI of Scotland became James I of England and moved his Court to nearby Greenwich Palace. This is an engraving from the end of the last century.

On the other side of the world in Australia, the game of golf took a little longer to become established and widely popular. The oldest club still in existence is the Royal Melbourne, founded in 1891, although the game was being played there and in Sydney for some decades before that.

The real explosion in golf's popularity came, together with other sports, in the second half of the nineteenth century. The continuing advances in technology gave increasing numbers of people more free time and money to spend. The discovery that gutta-percha made a tough and cheap ball meant that the game was no longer exclusively for the wealthy. The railways opened up the country and the game became accessible to more and more people.

THE UNITED STATES GOLF ASSOCIATION

The USGA was founded in December 1894 by Henry O. Tallmadge to bring some cohesion to the game. Earlier in that year, two separate Amateur Golf Championships of the United States had been held, one at the Newport Club, Rhode Island, and one at the St Andrew's Club, Yonkers, New York. Today the USGA is the governing body of golf in America. The rules of the game are updated every four years jointly by the USGA and the Royal and Ancient Golf Club of St Andrews in Scotland.

ABOVE: The earliest club still in existence in America is the St Andrew's club formed at Yonkers, New York in 1888. In 1892 the club moved to a large apple orchard in Weston and the members became known as The Apple Tree Gang. This painting is by Leland Gustavson.

LEFT: Bulldozers are the most important tool for moulding modern golf courses, but man power counted in the past. This is an American construction team, brought together to build a new course around 1910.

In the USA, the first documented club still in existence, St Andrew's, was set up in Yonkers, New York, in 1888, although the first one on the North American continent was the Royal Montreal in Canada, founded in 1873. New York City opened the first public course in 1895 and by 1900 there were over 1000 courses in the USA.

Despite a slump in the 1940s, the popularity of golf worldwide, and especially in America, has continued to grow throughout this century and today it has reached epic proportions.

RIGHT: Other commercial companies besides the railways were alive to the possibilities of using golf to increase their sales. This is an early twentieth century whisky advertisement. The caddy carries the clubs loose and the reviving bottle in his pocket! The illustration is a copy of Lemuel Abbott's 1778 engraving of William Innes, captain of Blackheath, and his caddy, a Greenwich Hospital pensioner. The bottle could not be identified as whisky in the original.

ABOVE: The Bovril Lady is a classic advertisement of its kind.

LEFT: Women golfers were used to promote items that were not aimed particularly at women, as this turn of the century advert shows.

GOLF BALLS AND CLUBS

The development of equipment in the game of golf had a significant effect on the game's rise in popularity. This is partly attributed to the introduction of new materials and the impact of mass production.

GOLF BALLS

The earliest known golf balls were made out of wood, probably boxwood, which would have split easily and not have flown very far. The "feathery", a clever invention but laborious to make, was mainly used during the seventeeth century. Pieces of cowhide were stitched together and the resulting case stuffed very tightly with boiled chicken or goose feathers. Then it was painted with white lead paint in a not very successful attempt to waterproof it. It is likely that the Dutch invented this ball, not necessarily for golf. Certainly the Scots imported such balls from the Netherlands before their own craftsmen took over.

The feathery was very hard and flew well but it had disadvantages. It was expensive, costing more than a club, was easily cut by an iron and did not perform well in wet weather because it absorbed water, despite the lead paint, and became heavy.

In 1848 came the greatest equipment revolution in the history of golf – the discovery

LEFT: The development of the golf ball from the feathery and the gutty *(left)* to the early rubber-cored ball of about 1905 *(right)*.

BELOW: Coburn Haskell of America developed the rubber-cored golf ball and the Haskell, as it was known, revolutionized golf.

HASKELL ROYAL 2/- EACH

OF ALL DEALERS AND PROFESSIONALS OR FROM THE SOLE MANUFACTURERS THE B. F. GOODRICH Co. 7, SNOW HILL, LONDON, E.C.

A sample ball sent post free on receipt of P.O. value 2/- from the manufacturers.

"I must have his name & address - he's driven beyond the limit."

ABOVE: A long-nosed wooden club by Simon Cossar of Leith. The head was secured to the shaft by a long spliced joint held by glue and tightly bound with whipping. It was the type of joint used to repair ships' masts. Simon Cossar was one of the best-known clubmakers of his time, working between the late eighteenth and the early nineteenth centuries.

ABOVE: This turn of the century club has a surprising hole in the middle. The idea was that if you were hitting your ball out of shallow water, resistance was decreased.

that you could make a ball out of gutta-percha. With this rubbery substance, golfers had a ball that flew further, was tough, didn't mind the rain and could be remoulded when it was cut by poor shots. It was also far cheaper than the feathery. The development of the gutta-percha ball helped open up the game. A working man could not afford to lose high-priced golf balls, and balls were easy to lose on courses which, if cut at all, were dealt with by a scythe and the cuttings left undisturbed.

In the second half of the nineteenth century, different compounds were used to make gutta-percha balls fly better. These new "gutty" balls were tougher and the heads of wooden clubs were made deeper and shorter to withstand the impact of the harder ball. They usually had an insert in the face to soften the shock and improved jointing was used between the clubhead and the hickory shaft.

The next improvement was the arrival of the rubber-cored ball at the turn of the century. This was developed in the USA by Coburn Haskell and was named after him. The Haskell, although softer and therefore kinder to clubfaces, was far more resilient than the gutty and allowed poor strikers to enjoy their golf far more because the ball went further. Others were more doubtful because the hard gutty balls were better to handle on and around the greens. The doubters were converted when Sandy Herd won the Open Championship at Hoylake in 1902, using one of the few rubber-cored balls then available.

GOLF CLUBS

Before 1820 the shaft of a golf club was usually made from ash, but then hickory, a North American wood, became popular because of its superior whip. The clubs were longer than modern ones, with long, narrow heads. The clubface was only 2.5 cm (1 in) deep. A set consisted of wooden clubs and one iron, used *in extremis* as it could easily destroy an expensive feathery. With the advent of the harder gutta-percha balls, the number of irons carried increased.

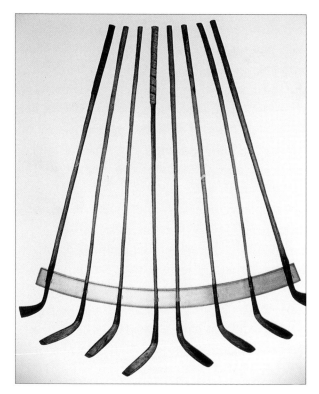

ABOVE: This is the first known set of clubs and is owned by Royal Troon. The clubs were discovered during renovations at a house in Hull, England.

In the early 1900s, ash was replaced by persimmon for the clubhead. This was another hard wood from America and, instead of the club being spliced and the head bound to it as before, the clubhead was fixed to the shaft by having a hole drilled in it and the shaft inserted. This method leant itself to mass production, which was enthusiastically pursued in America, so that by 1902 Britain was importing 100,000 golf clubs a year from the USA.

Greater length for the long shots is always an advantage and during the present century this has been the main aim of both ball and club manufacturers, even though short game skills pay off far more. But both very good and moderate golfers like to see the ball fizz high and far. The most significant improvement was the adoption of steel shafts, first in the USA in the early 1920s and then throughout the rest of the world. Until then, most clubs had hickory shafts; the terms wood and iron referred to the clubhead.

Compared to hickory, steel made the game easier for all levels of golfer. As a natural material, however expert the clubmaker, hickory varied in the amount of flex it had and it also twisted. Steel behaves much more consistently. Golfers could hit full out knowing that they did not have to worry about how their shafts would perform. With steel shafts, you got what you deserved, if you swung and struck the ball precisely. Hickory still had its fans, however; Bobby Jones, for example, stuck with his tried and trusted hickory-shafted

clubs throughout his championship career, though he later designed and used steel-shafted clubs. Despite the claims of manufacturers, there has been nothing dramatically new since the rubber-cored ball and the steel shaft. Even so, there have been changes which have helped great and lowly players alike.

Balls are made which do not cut, and other changes have concentrated on the way the clubface grips the cover. This leads to far more backspin for iron shots. Much thought has also been given to the aerodynamics of dimpling. As a result of developments in this field, the ball also flies further and keeps a straighter course, so veers less to right or left.

The club shaft has also received close attention from technologists and manufacturers. Many materials have been used, including aluminium and carbon fibre, the main aims being to reduce weight while retaining or even increasing strength.

ABOVE: Long-nosed nineteenth-century woods. The shape of the heads changed with the increasing hardness of the balls: (left to right) feathery, hand-hammered gutty, moulded gutty and rubber core.
BELOW: Some early clubs dating from the mid-nineteenth century; those with cut-off faces date from earlier still.

ABOVE: An 1850s type putter and ball.

BELOW: This savage-looking club was supposed to help the golfer cut through long grass. It is known as a rake iron and was made in the early 1900s.

ABOVE: Compare the early clubs with this set of modern forged irons.

Of course, much thought has also been given to clubheads. The central idea applies to all the clubs – putters, irons and woods. If you have a solid head on any of these clubs you have to strike at the so-called "sweet spot". However, if the weight of the head is concentrated more towards the toe and heel of the club, you have much more margin for error. Most would credit Karsten Solheim with introducing this idea with his Ping putters. It was soon extended to irons and metal woods by Solheim and others. Even so, none of these clubs is magic. Many golfers prefer to play with, for example, persimmon-head woods, forged irons and blade putters.

CLUBMAKERS

In Scotland the first clubs were made by bowmakers. In 1502 James IV purchased "golf clubbes" from a bowmaker in Perth. James VI appointed his own royal club-maker, one William Mayne, bowmaker, also of Perth. Throughout the eighteenth century there are written references to clubmakers, some of whom were also ballmakers, including the Dicksons of Leith, George and Henry Milne of St Andrews, David Dick of St Andrews and Andrew Bailey of Bruntsfield, Edinburgh. There is a 1770 reference to clubmaker Thomas Comb, also of Bruntsfield, who ran the local inn which was used as the Bruntsfield clubhouse. At the turn of the century and throughout the nineteenth, six families and three individuals were at the top of a thriving trade:

Simon Cossar of Leith (1776–1811)
Hugh Philp of St Andrews (1782–1856)
John Jackson of Perth (1805–78)
McEwans of Leith
Forgans of St Andrews
Patricks of Leven, Fife
Morrises of St Andrews
Parks of Musselburgh
Dunns of North Berwick

Hugh Philp helped found the Forgan business when his daughter married into the family. By 1900, only the Forgans and the Patricks were still active. The master craftsmen were put out of business by the development of the socket-headed clubs and the coming of mass production, necessary to meet the fast-growing demand.

GOLFING ART

Golf has attracted the attention of painters through the centuries. Indeed some of the earliest information on the game of golf and its forerunners can be deduced from paintings, particularly by the Dutch landscape painters of the fifteenth, sixteenth and seventeenth centuries. The artists may not always have been interested in the golf itself but rather in the picturesque landscape scene as a whole, and the challenge of portraying it.

The players may be no more than distant figures in a landscape; other activities go on around them.

The Dutch interior school of painters often depicted a domestic family scene. Some of these can be called golf pictures because a golf club or ball appears somewhere in the picture. There is, for instance, a sketch by Rembrandt in which a passing golfer is glimpsed through a doorway.

LEFT: "Golfers on the Ice near Haarlem" by Adriaen van de Velde (c.1660). The two kilted men in the foreground may be evidence of the golfing links between Scotland and the Netherlands at that time.

RIGHT: A young golfer of 1595, as shown in the top left-hand corner of the painting. Artist unknown.

FAR RIGHT: "St Andrews" (detail), artist unknown. There is controversy over the date of this painting of golfers on the Old Course. It is thought to be around 1720, but some experts have suggested it may date from the seventeenth century.

In Britain, mainly Scotland, golf was usually the main focus of attention in the picture. The first known British painting that is, in part, a golf scene, was produced by the Englishman Paul Sandby in 1746 and is set near Edinburgh. Portraits were commissioned by those who held important positions in a golf club. Today, many golf clubs display photographs of their captains through the years, but in earlier times a painting was the only option.

RED COATS

Before courses were properly defined in the eighteenth century, golf was played over whatever was deemed a suitable area of land, usually open to the general public. Red was the traditional colour for golfers' coats because it was easily seen and people going about their everyday business would know to look out for flying golf balls. This is why there is a preponderance of red coats in many of the golfing portraits of the time.

LEFT: "William St Clair of Rosslin" by Sir George Chalmers (c.1771). St Clair, captain of The Honourable Company of Edinburgh Golfers four times, was also three times captain of St Andrews. The picture shows him aged 70.

More recently, the emphasis in painting has switched to golf course landscapes, often with no golfers in the scene at all.

Apart from paintings, other collectable forms of golfing art include glassware, china and ceramics, statuettes, metalware and even the equipment used in the game, especially some of the exquisitely shaped woods of the nineteenth century.

TOP LEFT: Although this illustration appeared in the *Illustrated London Almanack*, 1864, it seems to be of a fierce game in Scotland. Whether women and children did act as caddies or whether this is a flight of the artist's fancy is open to conjecture.

MIDDLE LEFT: "A Grand Match played over St Andrews Links" by Charles Lees c.1850. The painting shows a tense match with the spectators almost over-whelming the players.

BOTTOM FAR LEFT: Lloyd George, British prime minister from , was a keen golfer. This watercolour by J. Michael Brown shows him at his club, Walton Heath, in 1915, watched by James Braid, the golfer, Herbert Fowler, the archi-tect, and Lord Riddell, the owner of the course.

LEFT: A series of paintings by Harry Rowntree was used to illustrate Bernard Darwin's *The Golf Courses of the British Isles*, pub-lished in 1910, and now a collector's item. This one is called "Portmarnock, Coming Home".

RIGHT: Various railway companies used the increasingly popular game in their advertising campaigns. The posters became art forms in their own right. Cruden Bay in Scotland was once in the forefront of fashionable golf resorts, until its hotel burnt down.

FAR RIGHT: This poster shows Gleneagles in the distinctive style of the mid-1920s.

RIGHT: This LNER poster advertises golf at St Andrews.

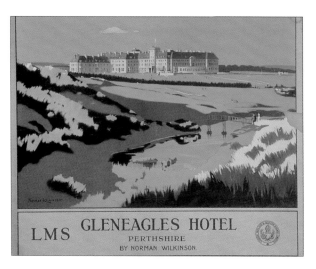

MEN'S GOLFING FASHIONS

When the popularity of golf took on the proportions of an epidemic from the 1880s onwards, what to wear was not an issue. Working men played in their hobnailed boots and nearly best clothes while everyone else did much the same, even though the standard of tailoring varied. The main idea was to look respectable. What you wore for golf was not much different from what you might have worn for a walk in the country or when taking part in a pheasant shoot.

As the game's popularity grew, the wealthier players, particularly, demanded more practical clothes. They took to wearing knickerbockers, which later became the famous plus-fours, and Norfolk jackets. These were originally designed as shooting jackets, with pleats at the shoulders for ease of movement – ideal for a golf swing, though Harry Vardon once declared that a tight jacket helped keep the swing in control.

The main aim behind the development of men's golf clothes was to produce garments that, as well as looking stylish, were comfortable and did not make the game more difficult. Serviceable shoes were a top priority, to provide a good grip and to prevent blisters and aching feet. As the customer base

LEFT: Golfers around 1800.

BELOW: This wood engraving of a match at Blackheath was produced by a local artist in 1869. The players are not wearing any special clothes, but one wonders if his stance helped the golfer.

RIGHT: A range of golfing footwear, about 1890.

BELOW: Plus-fours were popular in the 1920s.

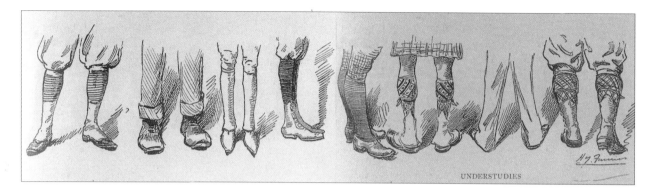

UNDERSTUDIES

ABOVE: Payne Stewart, well known for noticeable clothing on the golf course.

FAR RIGHT: Gary Player in black-and-white trousers, 1960.

grew, shoes became more sophisticated – spiked and usually made with materials of two contrasting colours.

Tweeds became the traditional golfing wear and remained so until the mid-1960s when more comfortable, casual and colourful clothes took over.

Special waterproof clothing for golfers first appeared in 1925. Until quite recently the materials used might keep out rain and icy winds but condensation inside meant that the golfer was usually damp in both wet and cold weather.

Now, modern "breathable" materials ensure that, like fishermen, cyclists, climbers and ramblers, golfers stay warm and dry.

These days, golfing clothes for both men and women are big business. Specially made shirts, sweaters, trousers, shoes, caps and visors are all available, the various makes endorsed by the big-name stars. You may even wear shorts, though these must not be too short and long socks finishing just below the knee are often decreed.

WOMEN'S GOLFING FASHIONS

In the last century women, like men, wore their everyday clothes to play golf. But for women this meant full length skirts, bustles, corsets and more or less elaborate hats – not the ideal golf wear. As a result, women were often confined to putting.

After World War I, things changed. As in everyday life, women's golf clothes became much less restrictive – a calf-length skirt, usually of tweed, teamed with blouse and cardigan plus beret or cloche hat and purpose-made spiked shoes. After the World War II, the clothes became more practical still: sensible skirts and sweaters and often no hat, until the revolution of the 1960s that affected men's fashion also took in women's golf clothes.

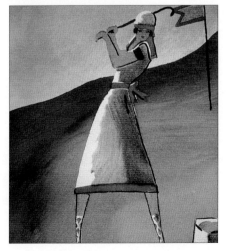

ABOVE: How did women manage to play at all in these clothes in the 1880s?

FAR LEFT: Women golfers, about 1890. The clothes are rather more practical than before, right down to the heavy shoes.

MID-LEFT: *The Golf Girl* by Louis Icart.

LEFT: Calf-length skirts arrived in the 1920s.

RIGHT: Golfing fashions really took off in the 1920s.

ABOVE: Karen McBeath, an RAF women's champion...

...and FAR RIGHT: Lisalotte Neumann wear the casual, comfortable clothes fashionable today.

Today there is very little difference between what men and women wear on the golf course. Rules for both men and women differ from club to club all over the world – in Germany, for instance, there are likely to be frowns if a shirt is worn outside the trousers, and many clubs in Britain lay down rules about golf course apparel. In most clubs, shirts and blouses must have a collar and sleeves. For women, shorts should reach down close to the knee and socks must show, even if ever so slightly, above the shoe.

THE "MISS HIGGINS"

Who Miss Higgins actually was is not known but she did have a wonderful idea. If she wore a long skirt that billowed in the wind, the results could be at least mildly embarrassing. So she wore a sturdy elastic band around her waist. When the wind blew, she pushed it down below the knees to reduce the billowing. In the last century, most women golfers went equipped with their "Miss Higgins".

THE GREAT COURSES

What constitutes a great golf course? It's really a matter of opinion. The club golfer and the top professionals will have widely different ideas. Leading golf magazines produce lists of regional and world rankings from time to time using differing criteria, but any list will usually include at least some of the key European and American courses listed.

Europe and America don't have the monopoly on great courses, although most are found in either one or the other. Australia, for example, has the Royal Melbourne, Royal Sydney and Kingston Heath. The Royal Calcutta in India, the Fujiyama in the shadow of Mount Fuji, Japan and the Gary Player Country Club, Sun City, South Africa, are also worth mentioning. Dubai has the Emirates Golf Club – a great example of creating a golf course against all the odds. It is watered daily with nearly a million gallons of water.

LEFT: The Swilcan Bridge at St Andrews with the Royal and Ancient club-house in the background.

FAR RIGHT: Augusta, the home of the US Masters, was designed by Bobby Jones and Alister Mackenzie to be a course "that offers equal enjoyment to all standards of player". It became the ultimate example of strategic design and the greatest influence on course design in America.

FAR RIGHT: Valderrama, Spain, was first laid out in 1964 by Robert Trent Jones. He revised the design in 1985 to make it one of the world's finest championship courses – the Spanish Augusta.

RIGHT: Turnberry, lighthouse and Ailsa Craig.

EUROPEAN
St Andrews
Carnoustie
Royal Dornoch
Muirfield
Turnberry
Royal Liverpool
Royal Lytham and
    St Annes
Sunningdale
Royal Birkdale
Ganton
Royal St George's
Royal Porthcawl
Royal County Down
Royal Portrush
Portmarnock
Killarney
Royal Antwerp
Falsterbo
Chantilly
Valderrama
Sotogrande
Club zur Vahr

AMERICAN
Shinnecock Hills
Augusta
Cypress Point
Oakmont
Baltusrol
The Country Club
The National
    Olympic
Harbour Town
Winged Foot
Pinehurst
Merion
Seminole
Pine Valley
Firestone
Southern Hills
Medinah
Oakland Hills
Champions
Pebble Beach
Dorado Beach
Cajuiles

FAR LEFT: Gleneagles Hotel from behind the 1st on the King's course.

LEFT: Royal Melbourne golf course in Victoria, Australia, is a composite of two courses. It was first used for the Canada Cup (the World Cup) in 1959. The best-known feature of the course is its lightning-fast greens.

LEFT: The Emirates Golf Club, Dubai, a haven of green in the desert, is watered via hundreds of concealed sprinklers and miles of pipes by purified seawater.

There are as many different kinds of golf course as there is terrain on which they are laid out – seaside with sand and coarse grass, flat Florida palmscapes, heathland, courses blasted out of rocky landscapes, parkland, courses carved into Japanese hillsides, inland layouts routed through gorse and pine forest. The list could go on to include modern courses that have been entirely shaped by machinery.

The vital factor common to all, however, is the talent and vision of the golf course architect and the men on the ground who interpret his plans. Over the history of golf, the men actually supervising the work have often vastly improved the architect's original designs. Until relatively modern times, the architect would arrive in, say, the Grampians of Scotland, at a site in Malaya or a new resort course around Palm Springs, stake out the ground, mark his ideas on the position of tees, bunkers and the greens, and then depart. The rest was left to the greenstaff who would labour long and hard to turn this very simple outline plan into a practical golf course. They are the unsung heroes.

Today, it is very different and architects may spend months rather than a few short hours on the site.

In America, course architects borrowed relevant ideas from the old Scottish links courses and introduced new ones of their own to suit their own terrain. Courses evolved along two distinct lines – penal and strategic. On the penal courses, often in the most spectacular settings, there is only one way to tackle a hole.

You need great skill and technique to succeed, and if you miss, it's severely punished. A good example is Cypress Point, California – at the 16th, if you get it wrong, your ball ends up on the rocks below or in the sea! On the strategic courses, the player must choose whether to take a harder, more direct route or a safer, longer way. Augusta, Georgia, is the ultimate example.

RIGHT: Pebble Beach, California, was sold in 1992 to a Japanese partnership for $500 million.

COURSE ARCHITECTS

Golf course designers were first called architects by Charles Blair Macdonald, the first US Amateur Champion, who discovered golf while attending the University of St Andrews in Scotland. He adapted the principles of a links course when laying out the National Golf Links of America, Long Island, New York. Great names in course design include:

Old Tom Morris	Hugh Wilson
Harry Colt	A.W. Tillinghast
James Braid	Donald Ross
Herbert Fowler	Robert Trent Jones
Alister Mackenzie	Pete Dye
Fred Hawtree	Jack Nicklaus
Jack Neville	

GOLF BEFORE COURSES

Before golf clubs were formed in the eighteenth century with their own premises and well-defined courses laid out with tees, fairways and greens, the game was played on appropriate common land. This was usually the strip of land linking shore and farmland – hence the derivation of the term "links". The grass was coarse and short and the sandy soil gave good drainage. There were no lawnmowers in those days and inland grass would grow too long to play the game comfortably and also meant a lot of expensive balls were lost. Inland areas were more often used in early spring or late summer when the grass stopped growing. Wherever they played, the golfers would encounter natural hazards – craters, uneven land, cart tracks. It's thought that sheep created bunkers, trying to shelter from the wind. The holes were roughly made and got bigger as the "course" became well used. On linksland, the players would take the sand out of the holes to make tees to drive off from.

THE GREAT MALE PLAYERS

The first golfer to be recognized as the best in the game was the St Andrews' professional **Allan Robertson**, who died in 1859. His death brought about the start of the British Open Championship, held the following year to establish who was the new greatest golfer. Played at Prestwick in Scotland, it was won by **Willie Park**; he and **Old Tom Morris** were the principal contestants for the title for the next few years until the arrival of Young Tom Morris, Old Tom's son. **Young Tom Morris** is still the only man to have won the Open four years in a row. His life was short – born in 1851, he died in 1875 – and we can only guess what he might have achieved had he lived longer. The ages of competitors were not recorded in the early years, so it will never be known for certain who was the youngest winner of all time but, at 17, Young Tom Morris is almost certainly the man.

There followed a succession of winners whom no one has ever called great, but the era of the Great Triumvirate was imminent.

J. H. Taylor won his first Open in 1894 and repeated his victory the next year. His great pitching made his contemporaries think him invincible – until **Harry Vardon** appeared.

That arrival was most emphatic, for Vardon beat Taylor in a play-off for the Open in 1896.

FAR LEFT: Tom Morris (rear) and Allan Robertson. This is a copy of an 1889 watercolour by Thomas Hodge, painted from an earlier photograph. Allan Robertson died in 1859.

LEFT: Willie Park from Musselburgh, first winner of the Open Championship, played over three rounds of a 12 hole links course at Prestwick. His score was 174. This oil painting is by John Bonnar.

LEFT: Old Tom Morris and Young Tom Morris. A studio portrait from the early 1870s.

RIGHT: J. H. Taylor, James Braid and Harry Vardon – the Great Triumvirate – in a picture by Clement Fowler shortly before the First World War.

ABOVE: Walter Hagen – "I never wanted to be a millionaire, just to live like one" – painted by Frank Bensing around 1957 from earlier photographs. It shows the serious side of this lively character. In his prime he would wear colourful clothes, plus-fours and black-and-white shoes, which at the time were thought outrageous by the more conservative people in the game.

Until tuberculosis weakened his form, he dominated the game winning four Opens in eight years and also taking the US Open in 1900. Eventually restored to reasonable health, Vardon won two more Opens, in 1911 and 1914 and remains the only player to have won it six times. On his two other visits to the US, he came close each time to winning the US Open Championship. While Vardon was dominant, Taylor remained a major force, eventually winning four Opens.

James Braid arrived a few years later and took the British Open Championship in 1901. For a while he was the greatest player in the land, winning five championships by 1910.

These three had contrasting styles of play. Taylor was extremely consistent in every department of the game but lacked elegance. Vardon had one of the most elegant swings of all time but, especially later in his career, was a poor short putter. Braid was perhaps the most exciting of the Triumvirate to watch, attacking the ball with fury.

They competed very little in the USA – Braid not at all – because in those days Britain was the centre of the world of golf. In the USA, the best players from the 1890s to the First World War were generally Scottish emigrants. This changed with the arrival of a the native-born American **Walter Hagen**.

Walter Hagen was first noticed when he finished close to the play-off for the 1913 US Open, contested by Harry Vardon, **Ted Ray** and the eventual winner, **Francis Ouimet**. The following year Hagen won; he won again in 1919. He came to Britain for the 1920 Open at Deal and finished well down the field, with only one round below 80. This very poor result did not in the least deter Hagen. The following year he competed again and he won in 1922. Through the rest of the decade he tended to win – as long as **Bobby Jones** wasn't in the field – taking four British Open titles in the 1920s.

Hagen won no more US Open titles – Jones was taking most of them – but in the US PGA Matchplay Championship he was outstandingly the dominant force. Between the years 1921 and 1927 he won five times.

Even so, **Robert Tyre Jones Junior** was the golfing hero of the 1920s. He won about half of all the events he entered from a mid-teenager until his retirement in 1930 at the age of 28. In the British and US Opens and the British and US Amateur Championships, he usually beat the field. Headlines featured "Jones Lost" as the sensation rather than the name of the winner. Between 1923 and 1930, he took five US Amateur titles and four US Opens. He competed far less in Britain, playing only four times in the British Open Championship. At the age of 19 at St Andrews, he tore up his card. On his other three entries he won.

Jones's greatest year was 1930. He thought it might be possible for him to win all the four majors open to him and so he did. Sometimes called the "Impregnable Quadrilateral" but more often the "Grand Slam", no one has since had even a glimpse of matching that achievement.

Jones had created enormous press and spectator interest in golf, which collapsed when he retired in 1930. In Britain, interest revived a little from 1934 when **Henry Cotton** took the first of his three British Opens, restoring a little national pride, but he did not really compete in the USA.

In America, **Gene Sarazen** arrived in a blaze of glory in 1922 at the age of 20, winning his first US Open that year and also winning the US PGA, a feat he repeated the following year, this time beating the great Hagen in the final.

Sarazen had a very strange grip, which was probably the main reason why he could not maintain the level of performance of his extreme youth. Yet he persisted, won his fair share of tournaments and reached a second peak in the mid 1930s. In 1932 he won his first British Open Championship, sailed back across the Atlantic and took the US Open a fortnight later, closing with a record 66.

In 1935, at the second US Masters, he played what remains the single most famous stroke in the history of golf. With four holes to play, Sarazen was three strokes off the lead but then holed his second shot with a wood at Augusta's par-5 15th. He went on to tie and won the play-off. That shot helped make the Masters the wonder tournament it is today.

Even so, with Sarazen and Hagen fading and Jones retired, America needed new heroes. Three were just over the horizon: **Byron Nelson**, **Sam Snead** and **Ben Hogan**.

Sam Snead will go down in history not only as the greatest player who failed to win the US Open but also as a man with a superbly fluent swing and as a prolific winner of tournaments. His main strengths were great length from the tee and mastery of the short irons.

Byron Nelson also appeared in the late 1930s, winning the Masters in 1937 and the US Open two years later. Even so, his most remarkable years came at the end of the Second World War. In 1944 he was leading money winner, but 1945 made him a legend. On the US Tour he won 11 events in a row

ABOVE: Bobby Jones, aged 14.

ABOVE: Gene Sarazen.

ABOVE: Ben Hogan.

and 18 in the whole season. He was nearly invincible. The following year he retired in favour of ranching and to be with his family.

Ben Hogan won nothing significant until he was 34 years old. He emerged in 1940 when he was leading money winner and, despite the interruption of the Second World War, amassed win after win. This was partly helped by the retirement of Byron Nelson, as Nelson himself had been assisted by Hogan's absence on war service.

Hogan had been a wild hitter, but he thought about the golf swing probably more than anyone before or since. His problem had been a low hook, but he succeeded in changing this to a low fade and his accuracy became legendary.

Early in 1949 he was so badly injured in a car accident that it was thought he would never play again. But he fought his way back and, although he did not play in the US PGA because the succession of 36-hole matches was too much for him, he took two Masters, brought his total of US Opens to four and won the British Open Championship on his only appearance in 1953. Only Jones has paralleled his dominance in the majors.

Bobby Locke was the first South African to make a real impact on world golf. Having destroyed Sam Snead in a series of matches in his own country, he decided to try the US Tour. In 1947, he arrived for the Masters and from then on was the man to beat. In a short season he finished second on the US money list.

ABOVE: Gary Player.

FAR RIGHT: Once a golfer, always a golfer – Arnold Palmer with a host of young admirers.

However, there were political troubles in the US and Locke played most of his golf elsewhere, winning the British Open four times with his extreme hooking flight shot and formidable putting.

As Hogan began to fade in his early 40s, other greats were about to emerge – **Jack Nicklaus** and **Arnold Palmer**, plus a very determined South African, **Gary Player**. Palmer came first with his win in the 1958 Masters. He became a superstar in 1960 when he took the Masters again and followed up with the US Open, after a closing round of 65. The equivalent of Jones's 1930 Grand Slam was a possibility and Palmer indeed came very close to the 1960 Open Championship. The early 1960s were his great years but he never won another major after 1964.

One reason for this was Jack Nicklaus, who deserves an equal place on a golfing pedestal with Jones. When Nicklaus arrived, Palmer was the acknowledged greatest and at this time a far more attractive personality. Nicklaus was sometimes charmless, sometimes arrogant, badly dressed and overweight. He was to correct all these things in future years and to become the greatest winner of majors of all time.

His first win at the majors came in 1962 at the US Open. Earlier he had won two US Amateurs, which today perhaps do not rank as majors when so many of the young turn professional so early. He had also, as an amateur, come close to the 1960 US Open. In that 1962 US Open, Nicklaus beat Palmer in an 18-hole play-off and in a way that set the pattern for what was to follow. Nicklaus was the new number one and

remained so until Tom Watson eventually displaced him towards the end of the 1970s.

Nicklaus won the Open Championship three times, the US Open four times, the US PGA five times and the Masters on six occasions, the last of these being a surprise victory as recently as 1986.

Player always had an ugly swing, born of the need to hit flat out in order to keep in touch with naturally longer hitters. He never became a dominant force in world golf but he was still one of the Big Three, just half a step below Palmer and Nicklaus. Even so, he beat them often enough, taking three British Opens, one US Open, three Masters and two US PGAs, a version of the modern Grand Slam, a record that Arnold Palmer and Tom Watson failed to equal.

Tom Watson was the young buck who supplanted Nicklaus when many before had tried and failed, including Gary Player, the small South African who made up for his relative lack of fire-power with a brilliant short game which has lasted to the present day.

For a while, Tom Watson was the dominant player in the British Open Championship, winning five times between 1975 and 1983. He was poised to equal Harry Vardon's six victories but one disastrous shot on the 71st hole at St Andrews in 1984 prevented a possible win and may have affected his future. He was never quite the same player again. The flow of majors dried up as did the tournament victories. He remains a formidable player

ABOVE: Tom Watson.

ABOVE: Seve Ballesteros.

FAR LEFT: Jack Nicklaus.

ABOVE: Nick Faldo.

ABOVE: Greg Norman.

through the green but is plagued by a suspect putting stroke, a vital part of the game where he was once arguably the world's best.

Stylistically **Lee Trevino** is without doubt the most unconventional of all the greats. He starts with a hooker's grip and then makes various movements to try to ensure he plays with a fade. The most extreme of these is a wide open stance.

Trevino appeared from out of nowhere to win the 1968 US Open. Viewing his playing methods, there were those who said he would never win another tournament. How wrong they were. Trevino went on to win another US Open and two PGA Championships, the last as recently as 1984. He also won the British Open Championship twice. In the twilight of his career on the US Senior Tour, he has been phenomenally successful.

Peter Thomson stopped playing the US Senior Tour prematurely, after immense success. He did not enjoy all the travelling. It was ironic that Thomson did so well in the USA when over 50, because he hadn't been deemed a success there in his prime. Thomson's real forte was links golf, which was the reason he was the man to be reckoned with through the 1950s in the British Open Championship. He had a simple but clear philosophy: "Hit the fairway, then the green and don't three putt." However, together with Jack Nicklaus, he was the man you could bank on to keep his game together in the tension of playing the last few holes of a major.

Severiano Ballesteros is a contrary example of a great player. He began as a very long hitter but was occasionally very crooked indeed. Unlike most golfers past their youth, he is as magical as ever on and around the greens, and is still the main attraction in Europe. His eventual golfing epitaph should shout that he is the most charismatic golfer ever; only Palmer is within touching distance.

Nick Faldo, by contrast, is "Mr Boring" but also probably the greatest British golfer ever. Except when he has a bad day, his game has no clear weakness. From the tee, he hits most of the fairways, is a superb bunker player and, though he often complains, is a very reliable putter indeed. His total of majors is now six, one better than Seve Ballesteros, and when the big events come round, his contemporaries see him as the man to beat.

Greg Norman is an enigma. In the majors, he has threatened to win many times. Having led in all four after the third round, he has won just two British Open Championships, despite holding the top position in the Sony rankings. With Arnold Palmer and Jack Nicklaus, he is the biggest earner in world golf, but that is probably no consolation for all the majors that he has either lost himself or had snatched from him by an opponent's fluke shot. The most outstanding feature of his game is that he is very long off the tee and straighter than any other big hitter. He also generates tremendous backspin with the irons and, as with all the greats, is a very good putter.

THE GREAT WOMEN PLAYERS

The standard of women's golf has risen enormously in the last twenty years. American players dominated the game for a long spell but far less so since Europe's best began to compete in numbers on the US LPGA Tour. While Europe and Australia are now producing world-class players, it is still true to say that the US has considerably more strength in depth.

In the past, women's golf was often dominated by just a few players. The first to make a real name for herself was **Lady Margaret Scott**. She was the best British player in the 1890s, retiring young after winning three championships.

Cecil Leitch, another Englishwoman, was the next to make a major impact in the early years of this century. She was followed by **Joyce Wethered**. During the 1920s, Wethered won almost every event she entered and then went into virtual retirement as she didn't like the strain of competitive golf.

Her only real rival was the American **Glenna Collett**, who emerged at very nearly the same time. While Joyce Wethered was winning her four British Ladies titles, Glenna Collett was on her way to taking six US titles between 1922 and 1935. However, in her few entries in Britain she failed to take the championship.

That honour fell to a very different American, **Babe Zaharias**. The Babe, as she was known, remains arguably the greatest woman athlete of all time. Before the 1932 Los Angeles Olympics, in the national championships, she entered eight events and won six of them, setting four world records in just two and a half hours – an afternoon's stroll of running, throwing and jumping. In the Olympic Games themselves, she was less successful, winning "only" the javelin and the 80 metre hurdles. In the high jump she set a new world record but was disqualified for using a style called the western roll, which was ruled "unladylike". Over 60 years later, this seems even more odd when everyone jumps over the bar backwards.

The skills of golf are more complex than those of athletics. The Babe turned to the game because she came from a poor background and needed to make money from sport. She tried baseball, basketball and tennis before turning her full attention to golf, which she seems to have first tried at the 1932 Olympics. She found the game much harder than other sports because gentle skills, rather than athleticism, are also involved, but she came through towards the end of World War II and went on to win 12 majors. On the new US

ABOVE: Cecil Leitch.

ABOVE: Joyce Wethered.

ABOVE: Glenna Collett.

ABOVE: Babe Zaharias.

ABOVE: Mickey Wright, who many would call the greatest woman golfer, lines up a putt.

ABOVE: Laura Davies.

Tour, she won about a quarter of all the events she entered before dying prematurely of cancer at the age of 42.

Patty Berg, in their professional days together, once described their encounters as "cat fights". In a main career that lasted longer than the Babe's, she won 42 LPGA events between 1948 and 1962.

Babe Zaharias, who had an extremely lively personality as well as wonderful golfing ability, left a big gap which was filled very differently by **Mickey Wright**.

Mickey Wright was the dominant player in the years 1958 to 1964 when she won four US Women's Opens and LPGA Championships and set the record of 13 wins in a season, and also the second best at 11. Her swing and hand action were arguably the best ever. Her eventual decline was due to a combination of loss of interest and some physical problems.

Kathy Whitworth, about five years younger than Mickey Wright, began to make an impact towards the end of Wright's best years. Her swing aroused no eulogies but it kept the ball in play, and she was one of the greatest putters ever in women's golf. By 1985, she had won 88 events on the US LPGA Tour, more than anyone else and more than record-holder Sam Snead on the men's circuit.

If **JoAnne Carner** had remained an amateur she might well have qualified as the greatest woman golfer ever. When she turned professional, she had five US Amateur titles to her credit. As a professional, she had a very

successful career and was generally thought of as the best player on the tour from around the mid-1970s for about ten years. She won two US Opens and tied in 1987, losing the play-off to **Laura Davies**.

Pat Bradley, now well into her 40s, remains good enough to qualify as a Solheim Cup player. She was at her best in the decade 1976 to 1986 and at that time became the leading money winner of all time.

It was, however, **Nancy Lopez** who gave women's golf the drama it retains. In her first full season, 1978, she won nine events and set the world of women's golf alight. She did more or less as well the following year and reached a career record of 17 wins in 50 starts – not quite as good as Bobby Jones, but not far off. Since those heady days her pace has slackened, due, she once said, to family interests, but she remains a force in women's golf.

ABOVE: Annika Sorenstam.

The present era has seen the emergence on the world stage of a few non-American golfers. With nine victories worldwide in 1996, Britain's **Laura Davies** claims pride of place, but Sweden's **Annika Sorenstam** and Australia's **Karrie Webb** have shot even more quickly to the top.

ABOVE: Karrie Webb.

THE GREAT TOURNAMENTS

The first major golf competition was the British Open Championship, played at Prestwick in 1860 to decide who was the greatest golfer of the day after the death of Allan Robertson the year before. Very few players entered for some years and there were equally few spectators.

How different it is today! From those extremely modest beginnings, the British Open, run by the Royal and Ancient Golf Club, may attract 50,000 spectators in a single day. That attendance can be so high is due to the policy of erecting large spectator stands. If you are at the Open, you have various choices; taking a seat in one of those stands to watch the golfing world go by is one of them. Otherwise, you can follow your favourite player around the course. Many watch the action on closed-circuit TV in hospitality pavilions and in the tented village.

Over the years, the British Open has become perhaps the greatest of all golf's competitive events. The field is more open than the other majors. The world's top players gain automatic entry, the less gifted go through a qualifying system. On rare occasions, a minnow may become a very big fish. This was the case in 1976 when Seve

LEFT: A presentation certificate with photographic portraits of Open champions from the early years.

ABOVE: Greg Norman wins the British Open for the second time, at Royal St George's Sandwich, Kent in 1993.

Ballesteros burst upon the scene. As a little-known nineteen-year-old he came close to winning the Open and was on his way in tournament golf. He won the championship three years later.

ABOVE: Billy Joe Patton, Ben Hogan, Bobby Jones and Sam Snead after the 1954 Masters ended in a tie between Hogan and Snead. Bobby Jones was largely responsible for initiating the Masters and Augusta National, the course on which it is played, assisting in the original design and later development.

The Masters is a very different event because it is the championship of nothing. It derived from a meeting of minds between Bobby Jones and Clifford Roberts. In the mid-1930s they started the Augusta National Invitational, which soon became known as the Masters. Jones originally saw this as a gathering of friends and acquaintances, both amateur and professional. In a much modified form, so it has continued. These days this is often seen as a weakness of the event because too many in the field have no chance of winning. The Masters has something offered by no other event – the drama of the last nine holes, which are the most familiar in the world of golf. The challenges are the same each year and are eagerly anticipated by the millions watching on television. Will a competitor find the water to the left of the 11th, come up just too short

of the flag at the short 12th and spin back into the stream, pull his tee shot at the short 16th into water, or misjudge or mishit his second shot into water at the long 13th or 15th? Many tournament titles have been lost or won on these last nine holes.

One of the main features of the US Open is the way courses are set up by the United States Golf Association. As at Augusta, the greens are always fast but whereas at Augusta rough is hardly a feature, it most certainly is at any course used for the US Open. The fairways are usually narrow and even the semi-rough is close-knit. When a ball drifts from the fairway it often settles out of sight in grass perhaps no more than a couple of inches deep. The wider rough is, of course, more punishing still. In either case, top players cannot usually control their shots to the greens.

When they miss, they are likely to find dense, if short, grass around the greens. This makes both chipping and the short pitch shot very much more difficult than it usually is in tournaments around the world.

A few players of no great stature, such as Tony Manero and Andy North, have won the US Open, and great players such as Sam Snead, Nick Faldo and Severiano Ballesteros have not. This is the only major tournament that no one has won more than four times.

The US PGA ranks distinctly lower than the other three majors, though other tournaments that have either hoped to supplant it or become a fifth major have failed to do so.

The tournament began during the First World War as a match-play event. It reached its peak during the 1920s as Walter Hagen cemented his greatness with an almost unbelievable winning run. No one before or since has matched his achievements. The US PGA was originally played over 36 holes of match-play, and in 1958 it became a 72-hole stroke-play tournament, largely as a result of the demands of television.

No one has won the modern Grand Slam of all four major championships, but the US PGA will arouse intense interest if a player already has the other three; otherwise it remains the major that commands the least interest.

LEFT: 1991 Ryder Cup, Tony Jacklin and Jack Nicklaus.

THE RYDER CUP

Samuel Ryder, a seed merchant from St Albans, Hertfordshire, England, was past his fiftieth birthday when, in 1910, he joined his local golf club, the Verulam. He was charmed by the game and took it up enthusiastically. He sponsored a tournament at his club and employed his own coach. When a team of American professionals played a team of British professionals at Wentworth in 1926 (to fill in time between qualifying for and the start of the Open), Ryder had already donated the Ryder Cup. The British won 13½ to 1½. Ryder was so thrilled by the event and by the chivalrous rivalry between the teams that he continued to support the British team financially for several years. As team selection had been haphazard for this event, records were kept

beginning with the next tournament in Worcester, Massachusetts, in 1927. The United States won 9½ to 2½. Over the years the United States came to dominate, until the British team included members from Ireland and then, in 1979, Europe. Since 1983, the competition has become even. The teams are chosen from the top players, who play for prestige only – and the Cup – and with both sides always determined to win, the battles are fierce and the rivalry intense, which makes this tournament probably the most gripping of all.

THE SOLHEIM CUP

Although the Solheim Cup was inaugurated only in 1990, it has already succeeded in capturing the public imagination. The top

ABOVE: Some of the American Walker Cup team who won at St Andrews in 1926.

FAR RIGHT: Harriot and Margaret Curtis.

women professionals from the US and Europe compete every two years. The first tournament was played at Lake Nona, Florida, and the US won by 11½ to 4½. Revenge was sweet two years later, when the Europeans won 11½ to 6½ at Dalmahoy, near Edinburgh. In later events the Americans have had the edge.

THE WALKER CUP

This competition between amateurs from Britain, Ireland and America was started just after the end of the First World War. The Cup was donated by George Herbert Walker of the National Golf Links of America, the 1920 President of the USGA. After a relatively informal match at Hoylake in 1921, the cup was

first competed for in the US the following year, the Americans winning by 9 matches to 3. Since 1924, the tournament has been held every two years, alternately in the British Isles and America. Several players who subsequently won the British or US Opens were members of Walker Cup teams, including Jack Nicklaus, Bill Rogers, Jerry Pate and Sandy Lyle.

THE CURTIS CUP

The Curtis Cup was named after two golfing sisters, Harriot and Margaret, who played at the beginning of the century, but the competion was not inaugurated until 1932 when the USGA sent a women's amateur team to Wentworth to play a team of British and Irish women amateurs. The American team has dominated the competition, although in 1986 at Prairie Dunes the British and Irish side became the first to defeat the Americans on home soil in any of the team competitions.

BASIC GOLF TECHNIQUES

A ll aspiring golfers need to practise their game and master the basic skills. This section covers the fundamentals for improving your game.

THE GRIP

Fundamental to a good golf swing is a correct and comfortable grip. There are three basic grips. The overlapping, where the little finger of the right hand is placed on the forefinger of the left, is the most popular. For the interlocking, the little finger of the right hand interlocks with the forefinger of the left. The baseball grip has been used by many players, though few of the highest class, because the right hand tends to work more independently.

BELOW LEFT: The overlapping grip.

BELOW MIDDLE: The interlocking grip, good for players with small hands.

BELOW RIGHT: The baseball grip. All ten fingers are in contact with the club.

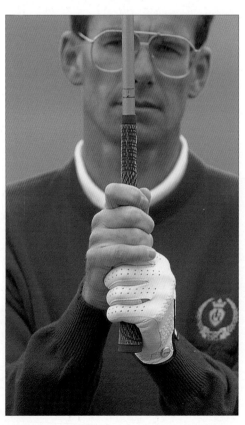

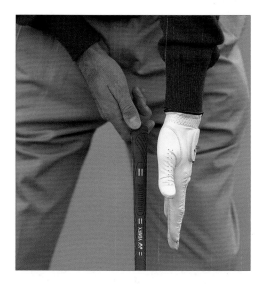

1 Support the top of the club with your right hand. Hang the left hand naturally down the side of the grip.

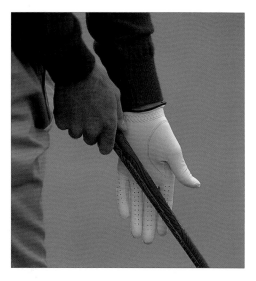

2 Bring your left hand forward and hold it against the grip so that the shaft runs from the fleshy pad in your palm diagonally down through the middle joint of your index finger.

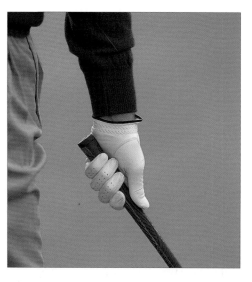

3 Close the fingers of your left hand around the club and let go with your right.

4 Your thumb should be flat on the grip, perhaps a little to the right of centre as you look down on it.

5 *(right)* Bring your right hand forward and lay the club in the fingers of that hand. Try to imagine that your right palm coincides with the angle of the clubface, in other words, is square to the target. Your right thumb and forefinger should form a kind of trigger around the grip, almost to the extent that you can support the weight of the club in your finger and thumb. At the same time, bond the little finger of your right hand in whichever way is comfortable, in interlocking, overlapping or baseball style.

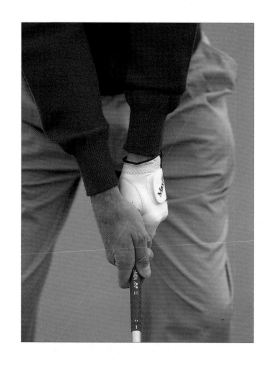

POSTURE AND ALIGNMENT

Correct posture and alignment are
fundamental to good golf.

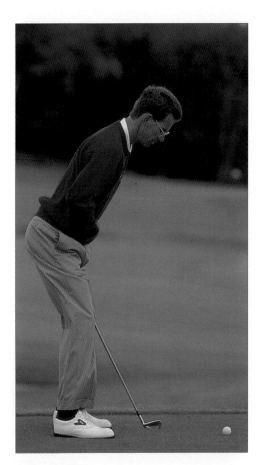

1 Stand with your feet shoulder-width
apart and pointing slightly outwards,
upright with a club resting by your side.

2 Bend forward from the hips. Bend
your knees slightly and stick out
your rear end. This should straighten
your back, which will then allow your
body to rotate properly during the
swing. Your stance should feel powerful
and balanced.

3 Take the club without altering any of
your body angles, and ground it.
This is now the perfect posture for your
height and build.

4 *(left)* In order to send the ball accurately to the target, correct alignment is essential. This involves lining up your body parallel to the ball-to-target line. Imagine a railway track running from your position to the target. The outer rail runs along the ball-to-target line and is where you should align your clubface. The inner rail runs along the line through your feet and ends up just to the left of the target. If you line up your feet and club along these imaginary tracks, you will be in perfect parallel alignment, providing you make sure that your hips and shoulders are also aligned and don't twist even slightly.

5 *(above right)* The ball must also be correctly positioned to ensure that the clubhead collects it on the ideal path, and this in turn depends on what club you are using. The relatively straight face of the driver means that you must sweep the ball away to achieve good results. The ball should be forward in your stance, roughly opposite the inside of your left heel so that the club reaches the bottom of the swing at impact. With short irons, on the other hand, the clubhead must be travelling downwards into impact to ensure that you achieve ideal ball-then-turf contact. Therefore the ball should be positioned back in your stance, more or less midway between your feet.

THE FULL SWING

Before attempting to hit the ball, follow your own pre-shot routine, which should include standing behind the ball and visualizing the exact shot you want to hit. Align the clubface and yourself, assume the correct address position and waggle the clubhead back and forth a couple of times to ease the tension in your hands, arms and shoulders.

The aim of the swing is to deliver the clubhead correctly to the ball every time. Anything that goes wrong with your grip, posture, alignment or backswing will be reflected through impact.

THE BACKSWING

1 From a solid address position, your main thought should be to swing the club smoothly away from the ball, keeping your arms and body working in harmony.

2 The clubhead moves away low to the ground, gradually arcing inside the target line as the body rotates and the left arm extends away.

3 The wrists should hinge, or set, in harmony with the swinging motion of the clubhead. Keep in mind that as the arms swing, so the body rotates. Each component part works together – your arms should never work independently of the rest of your body.

4 As you reach the top of the back-swing, your club should still be on line, parallel to the target.

THE DOWNSWING

1 The transition from backswing to downswing is critical. Try to start the downswing with a subtle move of your left knee towards the target, combined with a gradual weight shift on to your left foot.

2 The movement of your hips and torso automatically slots your hands and arms down into an ideal position to attack the ball.

3 The clubhead should be delivered square to the ball.

4 *(left)* Through impact, your hands and arms should freewheel up and around into the perfect follow-through position.

PITCHING

Shorter than a full swing shot, longer than a chip, a good pitch shot is essential if you are to improve your approach play.

Control, accuracy and judgement of distance are what matter most when you're homing in on the green. To achieve greater control, grip the club further down than you would for a full swing. This effectively shortens your swing back and through and ensures you won't overshoot the target.

The shorter clubs used for pitching and the fact that you have to stand closer to the ball mean that a square stance won't work. Adopt an open stance, that is, align yourself slightly to the left of the ball-to-target line, which will make it easier to deliver the clubhead square to the ball.

THE STANDARD PITCH SHOT – FOR DISTANCES OF 70–100 YARDS

1 Use your arms and shoulders to swing the club away from the ball in conjunction with the turning motion of your upper body.

2 Everything moves away together, referred to as staying connected in the backswing.

3 You must stay connected so that your body rotation controls the length of your backswing.

4 Similarly, in the downswing you should consciously make the arms and body control the swing together. Your hands should stay passive.

5 Accelerate the clubhead down into and through impact with the emphasis on the body, not the hands.

6 Practise with a number of clubs, including your 9-iron, pitching-wedge and sand-wedge. This will enable you to use exactly the same swing while varying the distance you can hit the ball.

The distance the ball flies should be controlled by the length of the back-swing, not by the force exerted on the downswing. Therefore the length of the backswing must vary, depend-ing on the distance to be covered. Again, practise with a number of clubs.

FAR LEFT: Hit ten half shots. Make sure the follow-through is as long as the backswing.

LEFT: Hit ten three-quarter shots. In both cases, note the average distance your shots travel. Then whatever situation you are in on the course, you will know which club to use and what length your backswing should be.

CHIPPING

Improving your short game means practising the art of chipping – the all-important shots that get your ball on to the green. The technique used for the standard chip shot can be used to good effect with a 7-iron, 9-iron and sand-wedge. Experience will teach you which to use and when.

THE STANDARD CHIP

1 As usual, your address position is vital. Adopt an open stance with your feet fairly close together and your weight favouring the left side. Remember, ball back, hands forward and weight forward.

2 Concentrate on a smooth take-away and be sure to keep your head still. Keep your weight exactly where it is.

3 *(above)* You need just a slight hinging, or setting, of the wrists as you complete the backswing. This effectively keeps the hands in charge, in an ideal position to lead the clubhead down into the ball.

4 *(left)* At impact, you should feel that the ball is compressed between the clubhead and the turf. It is this sensation of squeezing the ball forward towards the target that helps produce the necessary backspin. With a lofted club, the ball will check on the second or third bounce.

5 Your hands should stay ahead of the clubhead even through impact.

THE PUTT-CHIP

Part chip and part putt, this is a useful shot for hitting the green from under 20 yards over uneven ground.

1 Take an 8- or 9-iron and address the ball as though you were going to hit a long putt. Place your weight on the left side, the ball to be opposite your left heel. Adopt your normal putting grip. This helps deaden the impact and enables you to control the length of the shot more accurately.

2 Focus on making an extension of your normal putting stroke.

3 With a fairly brisk action, clip the ball away.

4 You'll find that the ball is lobbed gently forward, fairly low with plenty of run. It should race towards the hole, just like a long putt.

THE CHIP FROM HARD GROUND

This calls for precise technique. The sand-wedge is not the right club to use because it may cause you to clip the top of the ball. Choose a club with a sharper leading edge which sits tighter to the ground, such as a 9-iron.

2 Make a compact backswing with a hint of wrist break and smoothly accelerate the clubhead into the bottom of the ball.

3 The single most important aspect of the shot is to keep your hands ahead of the clubhead into and through impact.

1 Remember ball back, hands forward, weight forward? You need to exaggerate each of these by another 20% so that the ball is well back in your stance and your hands and weight favour the left side even more than normal.

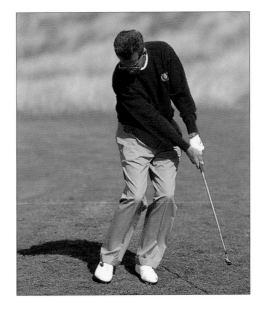

4 Achieving this technique through impact is the secret of successful chip shots from bare hard lies.

PUTTING

There are several different styles of putting, all with their devotees. Whichever you choose, your throughswing should be the same length as your backswing and you must accelerate smoothly through the ball.

ORTHODOX

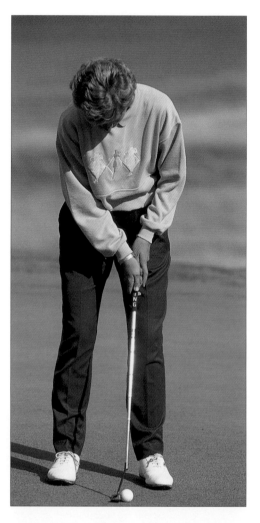

1 Place the hands in a neutral position, that is, with the palms facing one another. This is called the reverse overlap grip, and it encourages the hands to move as one unit rather than independently of each other.

2 Your posture should be relaxed – a comfortable bend from the waist with the hands and arms hanging down naturally and completely free from tension. Stand so that the ball is roughly opposite the inside of the left heel. Your eyes should be over the ball so that you can swivel your head to look along the line of the putt.

3 Note the imaginary triangle formed by the arms and shoulders at address. The stroke is a pendulum action controlled by the shoulders, with the hands remaining fairly passive.

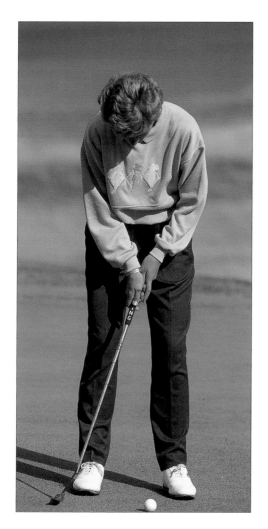

4 Try to maintain that triangle throughout the stroke from back-swing to follow-through.

5 Concentrate on trying to swing the putter-head upwards into and through impact. Having the ball forward in your stance encourages that upward strike and promotes a good roll. A descending blow tends to make the ball jump into the air.

6 Hold your follow-through position and don't look up too soon. Keep your eyes on the ground until the ball is well on its way.

THE ANTI-YIP STROKE

When the left wrist nervously breaks down through impact, the putter-face behaves erratically. This is called the yips. It can happen to anyone at any time, so it's as well to have an idea of how to deal with it.

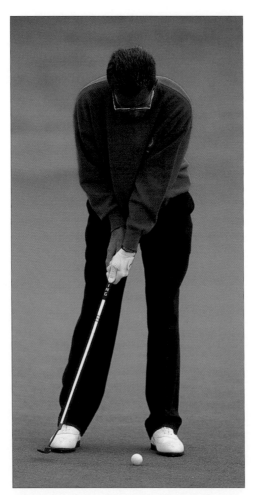

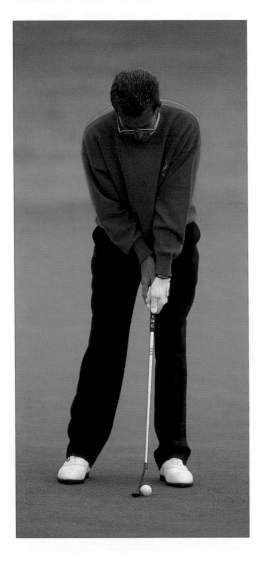

2 *(left)* The stroke is the same as the orthodox shot.

3 *(below)* The shoulders control the motion – simply rock them back and forth to regulate the necessary force in the stroke.

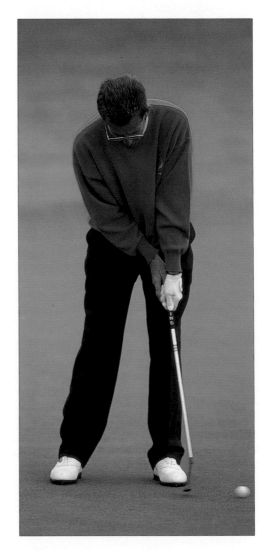

1 *(left)* A basic anti-yip technique is to grip the club with your left hand below the right. This locks the left wrist into position against the shaft of the putter and prevents any unwanted wrist action in the stroke. It has the added advantage of lowering the left shoulder, bringing it more into line with the right. It gives a feeling of the back of the left hand pulling the ball towards the hole.

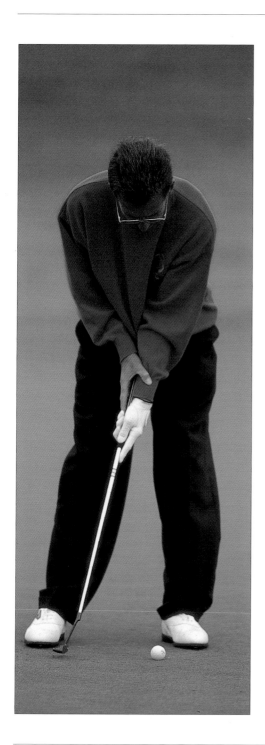

(left) THE LANGER GRIP

This is an extraordinary grip developed by Bernhard Langer to help him overcome the yips, and since adopted by many others. It is only suitable for short-range putting. Langer has now abandoned this grip in favour of the long putter.

Grip the club with your left hand well down the shaft. Clasp your right hand round the club and your left forearm. Make sure the grip pressure is light as any tension will destroy the smoothness of the stroke. The ideal ball position is opposite the inside of your left heel. Then concentrate on rocking your shoulders back and through. This should provide all the force in the stroke. There is no wrist action whatsoever. The putter should move back and through in a straight line with no interference from the hands.

(right) THE LONG PUTTER

The long putter was popularized by Sam Torrance in the late 1980s.

Hold the club at the top in your left hand and secure it against either your chin or chest. Grip the club lightly with the thumb and first two fingers of your right hand, rather as you would a pencil, and rock the putter-head smoothly back and forth. The weight and momentum of the putter does the work, your right hand simply guides the stroke.

COURSES PLAYED

U se the following pages to keep a personal record of the highs and lows of your game, where you have played and with whom, in which competitions. Keep a handy page of addresses and numbers of your golfing companions, clubhouses and courses as well as shops.

The Royal and Ancient Clubhouse, St Andrews.

Name ....

Score ....

Weather ....

Course condition ....

Number of putts ....

Driving ....

Iron play ....

ABOVE: Carnoustie in the spring.

Name ....

Score ....

Weather ....

Course condition ....

Number of putts ....

Driving ....

Iron play ....

Name ....

Score ....

Weather ....

Course condition ....

Number of putts ....

Driving ....

Iron play ....

ABOVE: The clubhouse at Sunningdale.

Name ....

Score ....

Weather ....

Course condition ....

Number of putts ....

Driving ....

Iron play ....

Name ....

Score ....

Weather ....

Course condition ....

Number of putts ....

Driving ....

Iron play ....

RIGHT: The 10th at Royal Dornoch.

FAR RIGHT: The 4th at Royal Birkdale.

Name ....

Score ....

Weather ....

Course condition ....

Number of putts ....

Driving ....

Iron play ....

Name ....

Score ....

Weather ....

Course condition ....

Number of putts ....

Driving ....

Iron play ....

PITCHING PRACTICE RECORD

Club ....

Length of backswing ....

Distance covered ....

Club ....

Length of backswing ....

Distance covered ....

Club ....

Length of backswing ....

Distance covered ....

Club ....

Length of backswing ....

Distance covered ....

Club ....

Length of backswing ....

Distance covered ....

Club ....

Length of backswing ....

Distance covered ....

Club ....

Length of backswing ....

Distance covered ....

Club ....

Length of backswing ....

Distance covered ....

COMPETITIONS PLAYED

ABOVE: The end of the British Open Championship at Royal Birkdale, 1991.

Competition played ....

Results ....

Self-analysis ....

Analysis of opponents ....

....

Overall view of event ....

....

Competition played ....

Results ....

Self-analysis ....

Analysis of opponents ....

....

Overall view of event ....

....

Competition played ....

Results ....

Self-analysis ....

Analysis of opponents ....

....

Overall view of event ....

....

Competition played ....

Results ....

Self-analysis ....

Analysis of opponents ....

....

Overall view of event ....

....

USEFUL ADDRESSES

Clubhouses and Courses

Other players

....
....
....
....
....
....

Shops

....
....
....
....
....
....

INDEX

Picture Credits

All pictures supplied by Michael Hobbs except the technqiues pictures by David Cannon, and pages 23, 24, 25 Visual Arts Library

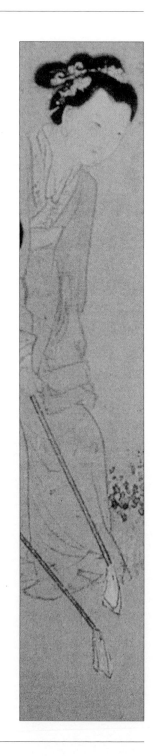